POPE BENEDICT XVI

THE EUCHARIST

Spiritual Thoughts Series

Preface by Cardinal Francis George, OMI

Introduction by Lucio Coco

D1213672

United States Conference of Catholic Bishops
Washington, D.C.

OTHER TITLES IN THE SPIRITUAL THOUGHTS SERIES

Spiritual Thoughts in the First Year of His Papacy
St. Paul
Mary
The Saints
The Word of God
Family
The Priesthood
Following Christ

Cover photo, *L'Osservatore Romano*

First printing, November 2009

ISBN: 978-1-60137-084-6

CONTENTS

PREFACE

anctity is unity with God through Jesus Christ. The Holy Eucharist unites us intimately with Christ and is the ordinary means of receiving Christ's life anew each day of our journey from Baptism to heaven. Those who receive this most blessed sacrament together know they are on the same path to unity with God, and receiving this pledge of salvation stirs up in their hearts the desire to invite others to the same banquet.

Pope Benedict XVI comments on theological themes related to the Eucharist and shares his own thoughts on this sacrament of unity. His synthetic grasp of the mysteries of faith brings into unity the many facets of what remains always a reality beyond our intellectual grasp. These reflections open us to the heart of our religion and more, because the Eucharist is at the heart of reality itself. Everything comes together in Christ. Each time we receive him under the forms of bread and wine, we rekindle our hope by placing ourselves within the moment when we will all come to grasp how God has worked throughout human history to bring good out of the evil our sins have caused.

The Holy Eucharist is the sacramental Body of Christ. It therefore creates the Body of Christ that is the Church. The Church cannot be understood apart from the Eucharist. The Eucharist unites Christ, the Head of his Body, with all his baptized members. In the eucharistic sacrifice, Christ is both priest and victim. Those ordained into Christ's Headship are to sacrifice themselves to make the baptized a holy people. The ordained priesthood cannot be understood apart from the Eucharist. Because the body received in Holy Communion is the risen Body of Christ, the seeds of immortality are received into still mortal bodies. Christ has promised that those who receive his Body and Blood will live forever, and we take immense consolation in that promise. The end of time cannot be understood without the Eucharist.

A deeper appreciation of the Church, of priesthood, and of the last things is stimulated in these pages, but all these realities are actually grasped in the proper celebration of the Holy Eucharist. Because he is a pastor and a theologian, Pope Benedict encourages the joyful and conscientious celebration of Mass, eschewing subjective aberrations that substitute ourselves for Christ.

Jesus promised to be with his disciples while they wait for his return in glory. The Eucharist fulfills that promise in a way that is unique and that is, like the Lord himself, a stumbling block for many. For those who, through God's grace, have access to the Lord's Real Presence in the Holy Eucharist, no words are adequate to express our thanks, and no thoughts are deep enough to plumb Christ's gift of himself. This book, however, is itself a blessing that confirms our faith. This is Peter's task and that of his successors in the unity of Catholic communion.

Cardinal Francis George, OMI
Archbishop of Chicago

INTRODUCTION

*In the Eucharist Christ gives us his Body and
makes us his Body.*

—POPE BENEDICT XVI

In this new volume of the Spiritual Thoughts Series
by Pope Benedict XVI, we find a collection of the
reflections and meditations of the Holy Father on
the Holy Eucharist, the mystery that completes the journey of Christian initiation toward identification with and
conformation to Christ and that "represents the center
and goal of all sacramental life" (*The Sacrament of Charity* [*Sacramentum Caritatis*], no. 17).

As the source and culmination of the life and mission
of the Church, the Eucharist is the sacrament of love: the
sacrament of Christ, who chooses to offer himself in his
sacrifice for us; and the sacrament of men and women who
through this sacrifice continually allow themselves to be
reached by this gift, allowing themselves to be transformed
by the sacrament of his Body and Blood, which in turn
makes them capable of giving themselves and their lives
for others. The Eucharist is at the center of an exchange
between God and humanity that did not occur just once in
history, but is renewed every day on the thousands of altars
on which the Lord again makes himself bread and wine,
again becomes broken in the Masses of the world, making

a gift of himself for all humanity. And once again men and women return to eat of this bread and drink of this wine, to nourish themselves with this mystery in order to give themselves again, to make themselves "bread broken for the life of the world" (Homily, October 23, 2005) and thereby to become participants in the labor and commitment of faith and life. "The Body and Blood of Christ," says Pope Benedict, "are given to us so that we ourselves will be transformed in our turn" (Homily, August 21, 2005). We ourselves must become the Body of Christ in order to make of ourselves a great offering that, like Christ's offering upon the altar, requires us to daily become lambs and victims, hosts in our turn, particles through which we must nourish others so that the mystery of his sacrifice and of our sacrifice may continue to be fulfilled today.

The Eucharist is the sacrament of union with the living God: "God no longer simply stands before us as the One who is totally Other. He is within us, and we are in him. His dynamic enters into us and then seeks to spread outwards to others until it fills the world, so that his love can truly become the dominant measure of the world" (Homily, August 21, 2005). It makes us participants in the work of Christ, who draws us toward himself and "makes us come out of ourselves to make us all one with him" (Homily, May 29, 2005). The Eucharist is the sacrament of unity, as St. Paul writes: "because the loaf of bread is one, we, though many, are one body, for we all partake of the one loaf" (1 Cor 10:17). Since we receive the same Lord and he welcomes us and draws us into himself, we are also one with one another. Yet Pope Benedict is also interested in highlighting the existential and practical consequences of this being nourished by Christ, of this feeding on him that leads to a process of assimilation of the person into Christ, which "must be evident in our lives. It must be seen in our capacity to forgive. It must be seen in our sensitivity to the needs of others. It must be seen in our willingness to share. It must be seen in our commitment to our neighbors, both those close at hand and those physically far away, whom we nevertheless consider to be close" (Homily, August 21, 2005).

We can take these "eucharistic thoughts" of the Holy Father as a guide in drawing nearer to the Eucharist and its mystery to be believed, lived, and adored. In this regard, Pope Benedict XVI never tires of underlining the importance of adoration, often turning to the Greek and Latin etymologies of the term in order to aid the understanding of it. The Greek word is in fact "*proskýnesis*," which indicates a gesture of submission. The Latin term "*ad-oratio*" instead indicates physical contact—a hug or kiss—and refers back to a loving context in which there is already an implicit relationship of union with the Lord, with him who is Love (see Address, March 13, 2009). In adoration we can grow and mature in the awareness that the heart itself of the Church, the heart of the life of every Christian, is essentially eucharistic in that it carries Christ within it. Just as Mary's actions become thoughtful and attentive when, pregnant with Jesus, she travels "in haste" to visit Elizabeth, who was already in her sixth month of pregnancy, likewise the Church is filled with concern and care for others and opens herself to the active experiences of charity because she feels a living bond with Christ. Her heart expresses gratitude because she perceives that there has been an encounter with his grace, and it is for this reason that we call this event the Eucharist, which means "thanksgiving."

Lucio Coco

THE
EUCHARIST

I. THE INSTITUTION OF THE EUCHARIST

1. *The sacrament of love*

It was there [in the Upper Room] that the Divine Teacher taught [the Apostles], opening their eyes to the splendor of the truth and giving them the sacrament of unity and love: the Eucharist.

> *Meeting with clergy in the Cathedral of Brindisi*
> *June 15, 2008*

2. *The Lord's Supper*

The Mass of the Lord's Supper remembers and celebrates the Last Supper, when Christ gave himself to us all as the food of salvation and the medicine of immortality. It is the mystery of the Eucharist, the source and summit of Christian life. In this sacrament of salvation, the Lord has offered and accomplished—for all those who believe in him—the most intimate union possible between our life and his.

> *General Audience*
> *March 19, 2008*

3. *The transformation of love*

By making the bread into his Body and the wine into his Blood, [Jesus] anticipates his death, he accepts it in his heart, and he transforms it into an action of love. What on the outside is simply brutal violence—the Crucifixion—from within becomes an act of total self-giving love. This is the substantial transformation which was accomplished at the Last Supper and was destined to set in motion a series of transformations leading ultimately to the transformation of the world when God will be all in all (cf. 1 Cor 15:28). In their hearts, people always and everywhere have somehow expected a change, a transformation of the world. Here now is the central act of transformation that alone can truly renew the world: violence is transformed into love, and death into life. Since this act transmutes death into love, death as such is already conquered from within, the Resurrection is already present in it. Death is, so to speak, mortally wounded, so that it can no longer have the last word. To use an image well known to us today, this is like inducing nuclear fission in the very heart of being—the victory of love over hatred, the victory of love over death. Only this intimate explosion of good conquering evil can then trigger off the series of transformations that little by little will change the world. All other changes remain superficial and cannot save. For this reason we speak of redemption: what had to happen at the most intimate level has indeed happened, and we can enter into its dynamic. Jesus can distribute his Body, because he truly gives himself.

Homily at Mass for the Twentieth World Youth Day
August 21, 2005

4. *True sacrifice*

"The Lord Jesus on the night when he was betrayed took bread, and when he had given thanks, he broke it, and said, 'This is my Body which is for you. Do this in remembrance of me.' In the same way also the cup, after supper, saying, 'This cup is the new covenant in my Blood. Do this, as often as you drink it, in remembrance of me'" (1 Cor 11:23-35). It is an inexhaustible text. . . . Paul transmits the Lord's words on the cup like this: this cup is "the new covenant in my Blood." These words conceal an allusion to two fundamental texts of the Old Testament. The first refers to the promise of a new covenant in the Book of the Prophet Jeremiah. Jesus tells the disciples and tells us: now, at this moment, with me and with my death the new covenant is fulfilled; by my Blood this new history of humanity begins in the world. However, also present in these words is a reference to the moment of the covenant on Sinai, when Moses said: "Behold the blood of the covenant which the Lord has made with you in accordance with all these words" (Ex 24:8). Then it was the blood of animals. The blood of animals could only be the expression of a desire, an expectation of the true sacrifice, the true worship. With the gift of the cup, the Lord gives us the true sacrifice. The one true sacrifice is the love of the Son. With the gift of this love, eternal love, the world enters into the new covenant. Celebrating the Eucharist means that Christ gives us himself, his love, to configure us to himself and thereby to create the new world.

General Audience
December 10, 2008

5. *New worship*

Holy Thursday is the day on which the Lord gave the Twelve the priestly task of celebrating, in the bread and the wine, the Sacrament of his Body and Blood until he comes again. The paschal lamb and all the sacrifices of the Old Covenant are replaced by the gift of his Body and his Blood, the gift of himself. Thus, the new worship was based on the fact that, in the first place, God makes a gift to us, and, filled with this gift, we become his: creation returns to the Creator.

Homily at Chrism Mass, Holy Thursday
April 13, 2006

6. *Living Bread*

On that night [Holy Thursday], Jesus goes out and hands himself over to the betrayer, the destroyer, and in so doing, overcomes the night, overcomes the darkness of evil. Only in this way is the gift of the Eucharist, instituted in the Upper Room, fulfilled: Jesus truly gives his Body and his Blood. Crossing over the threshold of death, he becomes living Bread, true manna, endless nourishment for eternity. The flesh becomes the Bread of Life.

Homily on the Solemnity of Corpus Christi
May 26, 2005

7. *Balancing*

As far as we can understand it, this is the sense of the Eucharistic sacrifice. To counter the great weight of evil that exists in the world and pulls the world downwards, the Lord places another, greater weight, that of the infinite love that enters this world. This is the most important point: God is always the absolute good, but this absolute good actually entered history: Christ makes himself present here and suffers evil to the very end, thereby creating a counter-weight of absolute value. Even if we see only empirically the proportions of the *plus* of evil, they are exceeded by the immense *plus* of good, of the suffering of the Son of God.

Meeting with the clergy of the Diocese of Rome
February 22, 2007

8. *Eucharist and charity*

"Charity"—*agape* in Greek, *caritas* in Latin—does not primarily mean an act or positive sentiment; rather, it means the spiritual gift, the love of God that the Holy Spirit effuses in the human heart, moving it to give [this love] to God and to neighbor (cf. Rom 5:5). Jesus' entire earthly existence, from conception to death on the Cross, was a single act of love, so much so that we can summarize our faith in these words: *Jesus Caritas*, Jesus Love. At the Last Supper, knowing that "his hour had come" (Jn 13:1), the divine Teacher offered his disciples the supreme example of love, washing their feet and entrusting to them the most precious inheritance, the Eucharist, where the entire Paschal Mystery is concentrated. . . . "Take this and eat it, this is my body. . . . all of you must drink from it, for this is my blood" (Mt 26:26-27). Jesus' words in the Upper Room are a prelude to his death and manifest the awareness with which he faced it, transforming it into a gift of self in the act of love that gives completely.

Angelus
September 25, 2005

9. *Mystery of death and of glory*

The Eucharist is a mystery of death and of glory like the Crucifixion, which is not an accident on the journey but the way by which Christ entered into his glory (cf. Lk 24:26) and reconciled the whole of humanity, overcoming all enmity.

Angelus
September 11, 2005

II. THE SACRAMENT OF THE EUCHARIST

10. Sancta sanctis *[the holy for the holy]*

By faith, the Eucharist is an intimate mystery. The Lord instituted the Sacrament in the Upper Room, surrounded by his new family, by the Twelve Apostles, a prefiguration and anticipation of the Church of all times. And so, in the liturgy of the ancient Church, the distribution of Holy Communion was introduced with the words *Sancta sanctis*: the holy gift is intended for those who have been made holy. In this way a response was given to the exhortation of St. Paul to the Corinthians: "A man should examine himself first; only then should he eat of the bread and drink of the cup . . ." (1 Cor 11:28).

Homily on the Solemnity of Corpus Christi
May 26, 2005

11. *Dynamism*

At the Last Supper, [Jesus] anticipated his death and resurrection by giving his disciples, in the bread and wine, his very self, his body and blood as the new manna (cf. Jn 6:31-33). The ancient world had dimly perceived that man's real food—what truly nourishes him as man—is ultimately the *Logos*, eternal wisdom. This same *Logos* now truly becomes food for us—as love. The Eucharist draws us into Jesus' act of self-oblation. More than just statically receiving the incarnate *Logos*, we enter into the very dynamic of his self-giving. The imagery of marriage between God and Israel is now realized in a way previously inconceivable: it had meant standing in God's presence, but now it becomes union with God through sharing in Jesus' self-gift, sharing in his body and blood. The sacramental "mysticism," grounded in God's condescension towards us, operates at a radically different level and lifts us to far greater heights than anything that any human mystical elevation could ever accomplish.

Encyclical letter God Is Love (Deus Caritas Est), *no. 13*
December 25, 2005

12. *Assimilation*

Christ gives us his Body in the Eucharist, he gives himself in his Body and thus makes us his Body, he unites us with his Risen Body. If man eats ordinary bread, in the digestive process this bread becomes part of his body, transformed into a substance of human life. But in holy Communion the inverse process is brought about. Christ, the Lord, assimilates us into himself, introducing us into his glorious Body, and thus we all become his Body.

General Audience
December 10, 2008

13. *Incorporation*

Here emerges the doctrine of the Body of Christ, because we are all incorporated if we receive worthily the Eucharist in the same Christ. Therefore our neighbor is truly near: no longer are we two separate "selves" but we are united in the same "self" of Christ.

Meeting with clergy of the Diocese of Rome
February 26, 2009

14. *Conformation*

"Take, eat. . . . Drink of it, all of you" (Mt 26:26ff.). It is not possible to "eat" the Risen One, present under the sign of bread, as if it were a simple piece of bread. To eat this Bread is to communicate, to enter into communion with the person of the living Lord. This communion, this act of "eating," is truly an encounter between two persons, it is allowing our lives to be penetrated by the life of the One who is the Lord, of the One who is my Creator and Redeemer. The purpose of this communion, of this partaking, is the assimilation of my life with his, my transformation and conformation into he who is living Love.

Homily on the Solemnity of Corpus Christi
May 26, 2005

15. *Dynamic presence*

We need a God who is close, a God who puts himself in our hands and who loves us. Christ is truly present among us in the Eucharist. His presence is not static. It is a dynamic presence that grasps us, to make us his own, to make us assimilate him. Christ draws us to him, he makes us come out of ourselves to make us all one with him. In this way he also integrates us in the communities of brothers and sisters, and communion with the Lord is always also communion with our brothers and sisters. And we see the beauty of this communion that the Blessed Eucharist gives us.

> *Homily at the closing of the twenty-fourth*
> *Italian National Eucharistic Congress*
> *May 29, 2005*

16. *Com-union [union-with]*

"Whoever remains in me," says the Lord, "will bear much fruit, because without me you can do nothing" (Jn 15:5). The secret of spiritual fruitfulness is union with God, union that is realized especially in the Eucharist, also rightly called "Communion."

> Regina Caeli
> *May 14, 2006*

17. *Holy Communion*

In Holy Communion . . . we can, as it were, drink directly from the source of life: he comes to us and makes each of us one with him. We can see how true this is: through the Eucharist, the sacrament of communion, a community is formed which spills over all borders and embraces all languages—we see it here: there are present Bishops of every language and from throughout the world—through communion the universal Church takes shape, in which God speaks to us and lives among us. This is how we should receive Holy Communion: seeing it as an encounter with Jesus, an encounter with God himself, who leads us to the sources of true life.

Homily at Vespers in the Cathedral of Munich
September 10, 2006

18. *In the Eucharist*

[Jesus is present in the Eucharist.] No, we cannot see him, but there are many things that we do not see, but they exist and are essential. For example: we do not see our reason, yet we have reason. We do not see our intelligence and we have it. In a word: we do not see our soul, and yet it exists and we see its effects, because we can speak, think and make decisions, etc. Nor do we see an electric current, for example, yet we see that it exists; we see this microphone, that it is working, and we see lights. Therefore, we do not see the very deepest things, those that really sustain life and the world, but we can see and feel their effects. This is also true for electricity; we do not see the electric current but we see the light. So it is with the Risen Lord: we do not see him with our eyes but we see that wherever Jesus is, people change, they improve. A greater capacity for peace, for reconciliation, etc., is created. Therefore, we do not see the Lord himself, but we see the effects of the Lord: so we can understand that Jesus is present. And as I said, it is precisely the invisible things that are the most profound, the most important. So let us go to meet this invisible but powerful Lord who helps us to live well.

Meeting with children who had received
First Communion that year
October 15, 2005

19. *Prayer*

Faith in Jesus, Son of the living God, is the means through which, time and again, we can take hold of Jesus' hand and in which he takes our hands and guides us. One of my favorite prayers is the request that the liturgy puts on our lips before Communion: "never let me be separated from you." Let us ask that we never fall away from communion with his Body, with Christ himself, that we do not fall away from the Eucharistic mystery. Let us ask that he will never let go of our hands.

Homily at Chrism Mass, Holy Thursday
April 13, 2006

20. *The First Communion of Pope Benedict XVI*

I remember my First Communion day very well. It was a lovely Sunday in March 1936, sixty-nine years ago. It was a sunny day, the church looked very beautiful, there was music. . . . There were so many beautiful things that I remember. There were about thirty of us, boys and girls from my little village of no more than 500 inhabitants. But at the heart of my joyful and beautiful memories is this one—and your spokesperson said the same thing: I understood that Jesus had entered my heart, he had actually visited me. And with Jesus, God himself was with me. And I realized that this is a gift of love that is truly worth more than all the other things that life can give. So on that day I was really filled with great joy, because Jesus came to me, and I realized that a new stage in my life was beginning, I was nine years old, and that it was henceforth important to stay faithful to that encounter, to that communion. I promised the Lord as best I could: "I always want to stay with you," and I prayed to him, "but above all, stay with me." So I went on living my life like that; thanks be to God, the Lord has always taken me by the hand and guided me, even in difficult situations. Thus, that day of my First Communion was the beginning of a journey made together. I hope that for all of you too, the First Communion you have received in this Year of the Eucharist will be the beginning of a lifelong friendship with Jesus, the beginning of a journey together, because in walking with Jesus we do well and life becomes good.

Meeting with children who had received
First Communion that year
October 15, 2005

21. *Journey*

Let us pray the Lord to help us in this journey that began with Baptism, a journey of identification with Christ that is fulfilled ever anew in the Eucharist. In the Third Eucharistic Prayer we say: "That we . . . become one body, one spirit in Christ." It is a moment in which, through the Eucharist and through our true participation in the mystery of Christ's death and Resurrection, we become one spirit with him. We exist in this identity of will, and thus we truly reach freedom.

Visit to the Roman Major Seminary
February 20, 2009

22. *Universality*

We greet the One who, in the Eucharist, always comes to us again in the name of the Lord, thus joining the ends of the earth in God's peace. This experience of universality is an essential part of the Eucharist. Since the Lord comes, we emerge from our exclusive forms of particularism and enter into the great community of all who are celebrating this holy sacrament. We enter his Kingdom of peace and in him, in a certain way, we greet all our brothers and sisters to whom he comes, to become truly a kingdom of peace in the midst of this lacerated world.

Homily at Mass on Palm Sunday
April 9, 2006

23. *Relationship*

The Eucharist . . . makes the Lord truly present in history. Through the reality of his Body and his Blood, the whole Christ makes himself substantially present in our lives. He is with us always, until the end of time (cf. Mt 28:20) and he sends us back to our daily lives so that we can fill them with his presence. In the Eucharist, it becomes clearly evident that our life is a relationship of communion with God, with our brothers and sisters, and with all creation. The Eucharist is the source of a unity reconciled in peace.

Meeting with the Special Council for the
Synod of Africa in Yaoundé, Cameroon
March 19, 2009

24. *The personal and social character of the Sacrament of the Eucharist*

"The cup of blessing which we bless, is it not a participation in the Blood of Christ? The bread which we break, is it not a participation in the Body of Christ? Because there is one bread, we who are many are one body, for we all partake of the one bread" (1 Cor 10:16-17). In these words the personal and social character of the Sacrament of the Eucharist likewise appears. Christ personally unites himself with each one of us, but Christ himself is also united with the man and the woman who are next to me. And the bread is for me but it is also for the other. Thus Christ unites all of us with himself and all of us with one another. In communion we receive Christ. But Christ is likewise united with my neighbor: Christ and my neighbor are inseparable in the Eucharist. And thus we are all one bread and one body. A Eucharist without solidarity with others is a Eucharist abused. And here we come to the root and, at the same time, the kernel of the doctrine on the Church as the Body of Christ, of the Risen Christ.

General Audience
December 10, 2008

25. *Practice*

"Worship" itself, Eucharistic communion, includes the reality both of being loved and of loving others in turn. A Eucharist which does not pass over into the concrete practice of love is intrinsically fragmented.

Encyclical letter God Is Love (Deus Caritas Est), *no. 14*
December 25, 2005

26. *Love of neighbor*

This sacramental "mysticism" is social in character, for in sacramental communion I become one with the Lord, like all the other communicants. As St. Paul says, "Because there is one bread, we who are many are one body, for we all partake of the one bread" (1 Cor 10:17). Union with Christ is also union with all those to whom he gives himself. I cannot possess Christ just for myself; I can belong to him only in union with all those who have become, or who will become, his own. Communion draws me out of myself towards him, and thus also towards unity with all Christians. We become "one body," completely joined in a single existence. Love of God and love of neighbor are now truly united: God incarnate draws us all to himself. We can thus understand how *agape* also became a term for the Eucharist: there God's own *agape* comes to us bodily, in order to continue his work in us and through us.

Encyclical letter God Is Love (Deus Caritas Est), *no. 14*
December 25, 2005

27. *Fruitfulness*

The Eucharist is our most beautiful treasure. It is the Sacrament par excellence; it ushers us into eternal life in advance; it contains the entire mystery of our salvation; it is the source and summit of the action and life of the Church, as the Second Vatican Council recalled (cf. *Sacrosanctum Concilium*, no. 8). It is therefore particularly important that pastors and faithful be constantly committed to deepening their knowledge of this great Sacrament. In this way each one will be able to affirm his faith and carry out his mission in the Church and in the world ever better, remembering that the Eucharist bears fruit in one's personal life, in the life of the Church and the world.

Homily delivered by satellite for the closing of the forty-ninth International Eucharistic Conference in Québec June 22, 2008

28. *Drug of immortality*

The Church Fathers have called the Eucharist a *drug of immortality*. And so it is, for in the Eucharist we come into contact, indeed, we enter into communion with the Risen Body of Christ, we enter the space of life already raised, eternal life. Let us enter into communion with this Body which is enlivened by immortal life and thus, from this moment and for ever, we will dwell in the space of life itself.

> *Homily at Mass in San Lorenzo*
> *International Youth Center, Rome*
> *March 9, 2008*

29. *Reconciliation*

The faithful . . . must seek to receive and to venerate the Most Holy Sacrament with piety and devotion, eager to welcome the Lord Jesus with faith, and having recourse, whenever necessary, to the sacrament of reconciliation so as to purify the soul from every grave sin.

> *Homily at Mass for the canonization of*
> *St. Anthony of St. Anne Galvão*
> *May 11, 2007*

30. *Perpetual Pentecost*

In order to grow in our Christian life, we need to be nourished by the Body and Blood of Christ. In fact, we are baptized and confirmed with a view to the Eucharist [cf. *Catechism of the Catholic Church*, no. 1322; *Sacramentum Caritatis*, no. 17]. "Source and summit" of the Church's life, the Eucharist is a "perpetual Pentecost" since every time we celebrate Mass we receive the Holy Spirit who unites us more deeply with Christ and transforms us into Him.

Message for the Twenty-Third World Youth Day
July 20, 2007

31. *Anticipation*

Communion, a fruit of the Holy Spirit, is nourished by the Eucharistic Bread (cf. 1 Cor 10:16-17) and is expressed in fraternal relations in a sort of anticipation of the future world. In the Eucharist, Jesus nourishes us, he unites us with himself, with his Father, with the Holy Spirit and with one another. This network of unity that embraces the world is an anticipation of the future world in our time.

General Audience
March 29, 2006

32. *Jesus Christ, future*

The Eucharist is also Jesus Christ, future, Jesus Christ to come. When we contemplate the sacred host, his glorious transfigured and risen Body, we contemplate what we shall contemplate in eternity, where we shall discover that the whole world has been carried by its Creator during every second of its history. Each time we consume him, but also each time we contemplate him, we proclaim him until he comes again, "*donec veniat.*" That is why we receive him with infinite respect.

Meditation during the Eucharistic procession in Lourdes
September 14, 2008

33. *Beauty*

This is the beauty of the Christian truth: the Creator and Lord of all things makes himself a "grain of wheat" to be sown in our land, in the furrows of our history. He made himself bread to be broken, shared, eaten. He made himself our food to give us life, his same divine life.

Angelus
May 25, 2008

34. *Hope*

How great is humanity's need today to rediscover the source of its hope in the Sacrament of the Eucharist!

Address to the Pontifical Committee for
International Eucharistic Congresses
November 9, 2006

III. The Eucharist and the Church

35. *Sacrament of salvation*

The Eucharist [is] the sacrament of salvation in which Christ becomes present and gives his Body and Blood as spiritual food for eternal life. A truly ineffable mystery! It is around the Eucharist that the Church comes to birth and grows—that great family of Christians.

Message for the Twenty-Fourth World Youth Day
February 22, 2009

36. *Eucharistic center*

Jesus' words at the Last Supper (cf. 1 Cor 11:23-25) are truly the center of the Church's life: the Church is built on this center, thus becoming herself. . . . The Church is built from and in the Eucharist and recognizes that she is the "Body of Christ" (1 Cor 12:27), nourished every day by the power of the Spirit of the Risen One.

General Audience
September 24, 2008

37. *Place of encounter*

God has a Face. God has a Name. In Christ, God was made flesh and gave himself to us in the mystery of the Most Holy Eucharist. The Word is flesh. It is given to us under the appearances of bread and thus truly becomes the Bread on which we live. We live on Truth. This Truth is a Person: he speaks to us and we speak to him. The Church is the place of our encounter with the Son of the living God and thus becomes the place for the encounter among ourselves. This is the joy that God gives us: that he made himself one of us, that we can touch him and that he dwells among us. The joy of God is our strength.

Homily at Mass in Our Lady Star of
Evangelization Parish, Rome
December 10, 2006

38. *Foundation*

We can see the Institution of the Eucharist as the true and proper founding act of the Church. Through the Eucharist, the Lord not only gives himself to his own but also gives them the reality of a new communion among themselves which is extended in time, "until he comes" (cf. 1 Cor 11:26). Through the Eucharist, the disciples become his living dwelling place which, as history unfolds, grows like the new and living temple of God in this world.

Homily at Mass on the Feast of SS. Peter and Paul
June 29, 2006

39. *Spiritual wealth*

The Holy Eucharist contains all the spiritual wealth of the Church, that is to say Christ himself, our Passover, the living bread come down from heaven, given life by the Holy Spirit and in turn life-giving because it is the source of Life for mankind. This mysterious and ineffable manifestation of God's love for humanity occupies a privileged place in the heart of Christians.

Homily at Mass for the canonization of
St. Anthony of St. Anne Galvão
May 11, 2007

40. *Body of Christ*

Paul holds that the Church is not only an organism but really becomes the Body of Christ in the Sacrament of the Eucharist, where we all receive his Body and really become his Body. Thus is brought about the spousal mystery that all become one body and one spirit in Christ. So it is that the reality goes far beyond any sociological image, expressing its real, profound essence, that is, the oneness of all the baptized in Christ, considered by the Apostle "one" in Christ, conformed to the Sacrament of his Body.

General Audience
October 15, 2008

41. *Sacrament of unity*

We must never forget that the Church is built around Christ and that, as St. Augustine, St. Thomas Aquinas and St. Albert the Great have all said, following St. Paul (cf. 1 Cor 10:17), the Eucharist is the Sacrament of the Church's unity, because we all form one single body of which the Lord is the head. We must go back again and again to the Last Supper on Holy Thursday, where we were given a pledge of the mystery of our redemption on the Cross. The Last Supper is the locus of the nascent Church, the womb containing the Church of every age. In the Eucharist, Christ's sacrifice is constantly renewed, Pentecost is constantly renewed.

Homily delivered by satellite for the closing of the forty-ninth International Eucharistic Conference in Québec June 22, 2008

42. *Network*

Thanks to the Eucharist, the Church is reborn ever anew! The Church is none other than that network—the Eucharistic community!—within which all of us, receiving the same Lord, become one body and embrace all the world. Presiding in doctrine and presiding in love must in the end be one and the same: the whole of the Church's teaching leads ultimately to love. And the Eucharist, as the love of Jesus Christ present, is the criterion for all teaching.

> *Homily at Mass for his own installation*
> *in the Chair of Peter*
> *May 7, 2005*

43. *Presiding in charity*

The Eucharist . . . is *agape*, charity, the presence of charity that is given in Christ. There must always be charity, the sign and cause of charity in being open to others, giving of the self to others, this responsibility towards the needy, the poor, the forgotten. This is a great responsibility. Presiding at the Eucharist is followed by presiding in charity, to which only the community itself can bear witness. I think this is the great task, the great question for the Church of Rome: truly to be an example and a starting point of charity. In this sense it is a bulwark of charity.

> *Meeting with clergy of the Diocese of Rome*
> *February 26, 2009*

44. *Being rooted in the Eucharist*

"Let each man take care how he builds upon it. For no other foundation can any one lay than that which is laid, which is Jesus Christ" (1 Cor 3:10-11). Being rooted in the Eucharist is indispensable to our work [in the Church]. The future scope of ecclesial charity must be based on the "Eucharistic measure": only what does not contradict, but rather finds and draws nourishment from the mystery of Eucharistic love and by the vision of the cosmos, man and history that flows from it, can guarantee the authenticity of our giving and provide us with a sure foundation on which to build. . . . It is precisely the Eucharistic inspiration of our action that will radically challenge man who cannot live by bread alone (cf. Lk 4:4), proclaiming to him the food of eternal life prepared by God in his Son Jesus.

Address to the Assembly of Organizations
for Aid to the Eastern Churches
June 21, 2007

45. *The task of Peter*

The Church . . . in her inmost self is a Eucharistic community, hence, communion in the Body of the Lord. Peter's task is to preside over this universal communion; to keep it present in the world also as visible, incarnate unity. He, together with the whole Church of Rome—as St. Ignatius of Antioch said—must preside in charity: preside over the community with that love which comes from Christ and ever anew surpasses the limitations of the private sphere to bring God's love to the ends of the earth.

> *Homily at Mass on the Feast of SS. Peter and Paul*
> *June 29, 2006*

46. *The Primacy of Peter*

This contextualization of the Primacy of Peter at the Last Supper, at the moment of the Institution of the Eucharist, the Lord's Pasch, also points to the ultimate meaning of this Primacy: Peter must be the custodian of communion with Christ for all time. He must guide people to communion with Christ; he must ensure that the net does not break, and consequently that universal communion endures. Only together can we be with Christ, who is Lord of all. Thus, Peter is responsible for guaranteeing communion with Christ with the love of Christ, guiding people to fulfill this love in everyday life. Let us pray that the Primacy of Peter, entrusted to poor human beings, will always be exercised in this original sense as the Lord desired, and that its true meaning will therefore always be recognized by the brethren who are not yet in full communion with us.

General Audience
June 7, 2006

47. *Treasure*

Indeed, the Eucharist is the "treasure" of the Church, the precious heritage that her Lord has left to her. And the Church preserves it with the greatest care, celebrating it daily in Holy Mass, adoring it in churches and chapels, administering it to the sick, and as viaticum to those who are on their last journey. However, this treasure that is destined for the baptized does not exhaust its radius of action in the context of the Church: the Eucharist is the Lord Jesus who gives himself "for the life of the world" (Jn 6:51). In every time and in every place, he wants to meet human beings and bring them the life of God. And this is not all. The Eucharist also has a cosmic property: the transformation of the bread and the wine into Christ's Body and Blood is in fact the principle of the divinization of creation itself.

Angelus
June 18, 2006

48. *Lens*

The Eucharist can also be considered as a "lens" through which to verify continually the face and the road of the Church, which Christ founded so that every person can know the love of God and find in him fullness of life.

Angelus
October 2, 2005

49. *At the origins*

The Eucharist is present at the Church's very origins [cf. John Paul II, *Ecclesia de Eucharistia*, no. 21] and is the source of grace that constitutes an incomparable opportunity both for the sanctification of humanity in Christ and for the glorification of God.

Address to the Congregation for Divine Worship and
the Discipline of the Sacraments
March 13, 2009

IV. Mary, Woman of the Eucharist

50. *Mary, Woman of the Eucharist*

Our Lady, called by the dear Pope John Paul II "Woman of the Eucharist" . . . truly teaches us what entering into communion with Christ is: Mary offered her own flesh, her own blood to Jesus and became a living tent of the Word, allowing herself to be penetrated by his presence in body and spirit. Let us pray to her, our holy Mother, so that she may help us to open our entire being, always more, to Christ's presence; so that she may help us to follow him faithfully, day after day, on the streets of our life.

> *Homily on the Solemnity of Corpus Christi*
> *May 26, 2005*

51. *The joy of Mary and the joy of the Church*

Mary went to see her elderly cousin Elizabeth, whom everyone said was sterile but who instead had reached the sixth month of a pregnancy given to her by God (cf. Lk 1:36), carrying in her womb the recently conceived Jesus. She was a young girl but she was not afraid, for God was with her, within her. In a certain way we can say that her journey was . . . the first "Eucharistic procession" in history. Mary, living Tabernacle of God made flesh, is the Ark of the Covenant in whom the Lord visited and redeemed his people. Jesus' presence filled her with the Holy Spirit. When she entered Elizabeth's house, her greeting was overflowing with grace: John leapt in his mother's womb, as if he were aware of the coming of the One whom he would one day proclaim to Israel. The children exulted, the mothers exulted. This meeting, imbued with the joy of the Holy Spirit, is expressed in the Canticle of the *Magnificat*. Is this not also the joy of the Church, which ceaselessly welcomes Christ in the holy Eucharist and brings him into the world with the testimony of active charity, steeped in faith and hope? Yes, welcoming Jesus and bringing him to others is the true joy of Christians! Dear Brothers and Sisters, let us follow and imitate Mary, a deeply Eucharistic soul, and our whole life can become a *Magnificat* (cf. *Ecclesia de Eucharistia*, no. 58).

Address at the conclusion of the Marian month
May 31, 2005

52. *In haste*

The Eucharist is the great school of love. When we participate regularly and with devotion in Holy Mass, when we spend a sustained time of adoration in the presence of Jesus in the Eucharist, it is easier to understand the length, breadth, height, and depth of his love that goes beyond all knowledge (cf. Eph 3:17-18). By sharing the Eucharistic Bread with our brothers and sisters of the Church community, we feel compelled, like Our Lady with Elizabeth, to render "in haste" the love of Christ into generous service towards our brothers and sisters.

Message for the Twenty-Second World Youth Day
January 27, 2007

53. *Like Mary*

When you [priests] take into your hands the Eucharistic Body of Jesus so as to nourish his People, and when you assume responsibility for that part of the Mystical Body which will be entrusted to you, remember the attitude of wonder and adoration which characterized Mary's faith. As she in her solicitous, maternal love for Jesus, preserved her virginal love filled with wonder, so also you, as you genuflect at the moment of consecration, preserve in your soul the ability to wonder and to adore. Know how to recognize in the People of God entrusted to you the signs of Christ's presence. Be mindful and attentive to the signs of holiness which God will show you among the faithful. Do not fear future duties or the unknown! Do not fear that words will fail you or that you will encounter rejection! The world and the Church need priests, holy priests.

Meeting with clergy, religious, and representatives of lay
ecclesial movements in Częstochowa, Poland
May 26, 2006

54. *Model*

Mary of Nazareth, icon of the nascent Church, is the model for each of us, called to receive the gift that Jesus makes of himself in the Eucharist.

Apostolic Exhortation The Sacrament of Charity
(Sacramentum Caritatis), *no. 33*
February 22, 2007

V. The Eucharist and the Priesthood

55. Amoris officium *[office of love]*

The ministerial priesthood has a constitutive relationship with the Body of Christ in his dual and inseparable dimensions as Eucharist and as Church, as Eucharistic body and Ecclesial body. Therefore, our ministry is *amoris officium* (St. Augustine, *In Iohannis Evangelium Tractatus* 123, 5), it is the office of the Good Shepherd who offers his life for his sheep (cf. Jn 10:14-15). In the Eucharistic mystery, Christ gives himself ever anew, and it is precisely in the Eucharist that we learn love of Christ, hence, love for the Church.

Address to the clergy of the Diocese of Rome
May 13, 2005

56. *Priesthood of the New Covenant*

The intrinsic relationship between the Eucharist and the sacrament of Holy Orders clearly emerges from Jesus' own words in the Upper Room: "Do this in memory of me" (Lk 22:19). On the night before he died, Jesus instituted the Eucharist and at the same time established the priesthood of the New Covenant. He is priest, victim and altar: the mediator between God the Father and his people (cf. Heb 5:5-10), the victim of atonement (cf. 1 Jn 2:2, 4:10) who offers himself on the altar of the Cross. No one can say "this is my body" and "this is the cup of my blood" except in the name and in the person of Christ, the one high priest of the new and eternal Covenant (cf. Heb 8–9).

Apostolic exhortation Sacramentum Caritatis
(The Sacrament of Charity), *no. 23*
February 22, 2007

57. *The Eucharist and the Sacrament of Ordination*

By virtue of sacred Orders, the priest receives the gift of and commitment to repeating in the Sacrament the gestures and words with which Jesus instituted the memorial of his Pasch at the Last Supper. This great miracle of love, which the priest is called ever more faithfully to witness and proclaim (cf. John Paul II, *Mane Nobiscum Domine*, no. 30), is renewed in his hands. This is the reason why the priest must be first and foremost an adorer who contemplates the Eucharist, starting from the very moment in which he celebrates it. We are well aware that the validity of the Sacrament does not depend on the holiness of the celebrant, but its effectiveness for him and for others will be all the greater the deeper the faith, the more ardent the love and the more fervent the spirit of prayer with which he lives it.

Angelus
September 18, 2005

58. *Entrustment*

The Lord entrusts to you [priests] the mystery of this Sacrament [of the Eucharist]. In his Name you can say: "This is my Body. . . . This is my Blood." Allow yourselves to be drawn ever anew by the Holy Eucharist, by communion of life with Christ. Consider the center of each day the possibility to celebrate the Eucharist worthily. Lead people ever anew to this mystery. Help them, starting from this, to bring the peace of Christ into the world.

Homily at Mass and priestly ordinations on Pentecost
May 15, 2005

59. *Builders*

Priests and the faithful alike are called to rediscover the Eucharist as the center of their existence, acquiring at that *great school of peace* a deep sense of their commitments and a powerful appeal to become promoters of dialogue and communion (cf. *Mane Nobiscum Domine*, no. 27).

Address to the bishops of the Congo
on their ad limina *visit*
February 6, 2006

60. *Eucharistic love*

At the center of every Christian community is the Eucharist, the source and summit of the life of the Church. Whoever places himself at the service of the Gospel, if he lives the Eucharist, makes progress in love of God and neighbor and thus contributes to building the Church as communion. We can affirm that the "Eucharistic love" motivates and founds the vocational activity of the whole Church, because, as I wrote in the Encyclical *Deus Caritas Est*, vocations to the priesthood and to other ministries and services flourish within the people of God wherever there are those in whom Christ can be seen through his Word, in the sacraments and especially in the Eucharist.

Message for the Forty-Fourth
World Day of Prayer for Vocations
February 10, 2007

61. *Won over*

Priests, like every baptized person, live by Eucharistic communion with the Lord. It is impossible to receive the Lord every day, taking his Body and Blood into our hands, pronouncing the tremendous and wonderful words "This is my Body, this is my Blood," without letting ourselves be seized by him, without letting ourselves be won over by fascination for him, without letting his infinite love change us from within. May the Eucharist become a school of life for you [priests] in which Jesus' sacrifice on the Cross teaches you to make a total gift of yourselves to your brethren.

Address to the Pontifical Ecclesial Academy
June 9, 2008

62. "Adoro te devote, latens Deitas" *["Hidden God, devoutly I adore thee"]*

We priests of the New Covenant . . . are every day witnesses and ministers of the "epiphany" of Jesus Christ in the Holy Eucharist. The Church celebrates all the mysteries of the Lord in this most holy and most humble Sacrament in which he both reveals and conceals his glory. "*Adoro te devote, latens Deitas*"—in adoration, thus we pray along with St. Thomas Aquinas.

Homily at Mass on the Feast of the Epiphany
January 6, 2009

63. *The daily Eucharist*

The Holy Eucharist, in which the sacrifice of Jesus on the Cross remains continually present, truly present among us, is rightly at the center of priestly life. And with this as our starting point, we also learn what celebrating the Eucharist properly means: it is an encounter with the Lord, who strips himself of his divine glory for our sake, allows himself be humiliated to the point of death on the Cross and thus gives himself to each one of us. The daily Eucharist is very important for the priest. In it he exposes himself ever anew to this mystery; ever anew he puts himself in God's hands, experiencing at the same time the joy of knowing that He is present, receives me, ever anew raises and supports me, gives me his hand, himself. The Eucharist must become for us a school of life in which we learn to give our lives. Life is not only given at the moment of death and not only in the manner of martyrdom. We must give it day by day.

Homily at Mass for the ordination of
priests to the Diocese of Rome
May 7, 2006

64. *The eucharistic celebration*

The ministerial priesthood involves a profound bond with Christ, who gives himself to us in the Eucharist. When the celebration of the Eucharist truly becomes the center of your priestly life, it will then also become the center of your ecclesial mission. In effect, Christ calls us throughout our lives to participate in his mission, to be witnesses, so that his Word may be proclaimed to all. In the celebration of this sacrament in the name and person of the Lord, it is not the person of the priest who should be put at the forefront: he is a servant, a humble instrument referring back to Christ, since it is Christ who offers himself in sacrifice for the salvation of the world.

Speech
March 19, 2009

65. *To seminarians*

I would say . . . that it is also important in the life of pastors of the Church, in the daily life of the priest, to preserve as far as possible a certain order. You should never skip Mass—a day without the Eucharist is incomplete—and thus already at the seminary we grow up with this daily liturgy. It seems to me very important that we feel the need to be with the Lord in the Eucharist, not as a professional obligation but truly as an interiorly felt duty, so that the Eucharist should never be missed.

Visit to the Roman Major Seminary
February 17, 2007

66. *To ordinands*

To be his worthy ministers, you must ceaselessly nourish yourselves with the Eucharist, source and summit of Christian life. In approaching the altar, your daily school of holiness, of communion with Jesus, of the way of entering into his sentiments in order to renew the sacrifice of the Cross, you will increasingly discover the richness and tenderness of the love of the divine Teacher, who today is calling you to a closer friendship with him. If you listen docilely to him, if you follow him faithfully, you will learn to express in your life and in your pastoral ministry his love and his passion for the salvation of souls. With Jesus' help, dear Ordinands, each one of you will become a Good Shepherd, ready, if necessary, to lay down your life for him.

Homily at Mass for the ordination
of priests to the Diocese of Rome
April 29, 2007

67. *The bishop*

Est amoris officium pascere dominicum gregem [it is a work of love to shepherd the flock of the Lord]: still today this wonderful intuition of the Bishop Augustine (*In ev. Jo. 123, 5: PL 35, 1967*) is a great encouragement to us Bishops, committed to the care of the flock that does not belong to us but to the Lord. In fulfilling his mandate, we seek to protect his flock, to feed it and to lead it to him, the true Good Shepherd, who wishes the salvation of all. Feeding the Lord's flock, therefore, is a ministry of vigilant love that demands our total dedication, to the last drop of energy and, if necessary, the sacrifice of our lives. It is above all the Eucharist which is the source and secret of the ongoing dynamism of our mission. In fact, in his ecclesial life, the Bishop is configured to the image of Christ, who nourishes us with his Flesh and Blood. From the Eucharist the Pastor draws the power to exercise that special pastoral charity which consists in dispensing the food of truth to the Christian people.

> *Address to the eleventh ordinary council*
> *of the General Synod of Bishops*
> *June 1, 2006*

VI. THE EUCHARIST AND MARRIAGE

68. *Marriage*

[Christ our Lord] has bequeathed to his disciples a golden rule to abide by in one's own life: the new commandment of love. Through the Gospel and the Sacraments, especially the Most Holy Eucharist, Christ continues to transmit to the Church the Love that he lived, even to death and death on a Cross. It is very significant, in this regard, that the Liturgy provides for the celebration of the Sacrament of Marriage in the heart of the Eucharistic celebration. This points to the profound bond that unites the two Sacraments. The spouses, in their daily life, must draw inspiration for their behavior from the example of Christ who "loved the Church and gave himself up for her" (Eph 5:25): this supreme act of love is represented in every Eucharistic celebration. It will thus be appropriate for the pastoral care of the family to stress this important sacramental fact as its fundamental reference point. Those who attend Mass—and it is also necessary to make the celebration of it easier for migrants and itinerant people—find in the Eucharist a very strong reference to their own family, to their own marriage, and are encouraged to live their situation in the perspective of faith, seeking in divine grace the necessary strength to succeed.

Address to consecrated virgins
May 15, 2008

69. *The marriage bond and Eucharistic unity*

The Eucharist, as the sacrament of charity, has a particular relationship with the love of man and woman united in marriage. . . . The Eucharist inexhaustibly strengthens the indissoluble unity and love of every Christian marriage. By the power of the sacrament, the marriage bond is intrinsically linked to the eucharistic unity of Christ the Bridegroom and his Bride, the Church (cf. Eph 5:31-32). The mutual consent that husband and wife exchange in Christ, which establishes them as a community of life and love, also has a eucharistic dimension. Indeed, in the theology of St. Paul, conjugal love is a sacramental sign of Christ's love for his Church, a love culminating in the Cross, the expression of his "marriage" with humanity and at the same time the origin and heart of the Eucharist.

Apostolic exhortation Sacramentum Caritatis
(The Sacrament of Charity), *no. 27*
February 22, 2007

VI. THE EUCHARIST AND MARRIAGE • 51

70. *The question of Communion for divorced faithful*

Two aspects are very important. The first: even if these people [who are divorced] cannot go to sacramental Communion, they are not excluded from the love of the Church or from the love of Christ. A Eucharist without immediate sacramental Communion is not of course complete; it lacks an essential dimension. Nonetheless, it is also true that taking part in the Eucharist without Eucharistic Communion is not the same as nothing; it still means being involved in the mystery of the Cross and Resurrection of Christ. It is still participating in the great Sacrament in its spiritual and pneumatic dimensions, and also in its ecclesial dimension, although this is not strictly sacramental. And since it is the Sacrament of Christ's passion, the suffering Christ embraces these people in a special way and communicates with them in another way differently, so that they may feel embraced by the Crucified Lord who fell to the ground and died and suffered for them and with them. Consequently, they must be made to understand that even if, unfortunately, a fundamental dimension is absent, they are not excluded from the great mystery of the Eucharist or from the love of Christ who is present in it. This seems to me important, just as it is important that the parish priest and the parish community make these people realize that on the one hand they must respect the indissolubility of the Sacrament, and on the other, that we love these people who are also suffering for us. Moreover, we must suffer with them, because they are bearing an important witness and because we know that the moment when one gives in "out of love," one wrongs the Sacrament itself and the indissolubility appears less and less true.

Meeting with clergy of the Diocese of Aosta, Italy
July 25, 2005

71. *Communion of desire*

Despite our weakness and sin, Christ wants to make his dwelling place in us. This is why we must do everything in our power to receive him with a pure heart, continuously rediscovering through the Sacrament of forgiveness that purity which sin has stained, "that [our] minds be attuned to [our] voices" (cf. *Sacrosanctum Concilium*, no. 11), according to the Council's invitation. Sin, in fact, especially serious sin, impedes the action of Eucharistic grace within us. Moreover, those who cannot receive Communion because of their situation will find a saving power and effectiveness in a Communion of desire and from participation at the Eucharist.

Homily delivered by satellite for the closing of the forty-ninth International Eucharistic Conference in Québec
June 22, 2008

VII. THE EUCHARISTIC CELEBRATION

Celebrating

72. Lex orandi e lex credendi *[the law of prayer and the law of faith]*

We must learn to celebrate the Eucharist, to learn to know intimately Jesus Christ, the God with the human face, and really come into contact with him. We must learn to listen to him and learn to let him enter into us. Sacramental Communion is precisely this interpenetration between two persons. I do not take a piece of bread or meat, I take or open my heart so that the Risen One may enter the context of my being, so that he may be within me and not only outside me. In this way he speaks within me and transforms my being, giving me the meaning of justice, the dynamism of justice and zeal for the Gospel. This celebration, at which God not only comes close to us but also enters the very fabric of our existence, is fundamental to being able truly to live with God and for God and to carry the light of God in this world.

Meeting with clergy of the Diocese of Rome
February 26, 2009

73. *With a prayerful attitude*

We celebrate [the Eucharist] well if we celebrate it with a "prayerful" attitude, uniting ourselves with the Mystery of Christ and his exchange as Son with the Father. If we celebrate the Eucharist in this way, first as listening and then as a response, hence, as prayer, using the words pointed out to us by the Holy Spirit, then we are celebrating it well. And through our prayer in common, people are attracted to joining the ranks of God's children.

Meeting with the clergy of the Diocese of Rome
February 22, 2007

74. Ars celebrandi *[art of celebrating]*

We [priests] must never do this [celebrate the Mass daily] merely out of routine, as "something that I have to do," but rather "from within"! Let us identify with the words and actions, and with the event that is really present there! If we celebrate Mass prayerfully, if our saying "this is my body" is born from our communion with Jesus Christ, who has laid his hands upon us and authorized us to speak with his own "I," if we celebrate the Eucharist with intimate participation in faith and prayer, then it is not simply an external duty; then the *ars celebrandi* comes naturally, because it consists in celebrating from the Lord's perspective and in communion with him, and hence in the way that best serves the people. Then we ourselves are constantly enriched and at the same time, we hand on to others something more than what is ours, that is to say: the Lord's presence.

Meeting with clergy in Bavaria, Germany
September 14, 2006

THE LITURGY OF THE EUCHARIST

75. *The Church's Liturgy*

In the Eucharist we receive something that we cannot do, but instead enter something greater that becomes our own, precisely when we give ourselves to this thing that is greater, truly seeking to celebrate the Liturgy as the Church's Liturgy.

Meeting with the bishops of Switzerland
November 7, 2006

76. *In fullness*

Every time the Mass is celebrated, every time Christ makes himself sacramentally present in his Church, the work of our salvation is accomplished. Hence to celebrate the Eucharist means to recognize that God alone has the power to grant us the fullness of joy and teach us true values, eternal values that will never pass away. God is present on the altar, but he is also present on the altar of our heart when, as we receive communion, we receive him in the sacrament of the Eucharist. He alone teaches us to shun idols, the illusions of our minds.

Homily at Mass in Lourdes, France
September 13, 2008

77. *Table of the Word and the Body of Christ*

We are always aware of the close connection that exists between the proclamation of the Word of God and the Eucharistic sacrifice: it is the Mystery itself that is offered for our contemplation. This is why "the Church," as the Second Vatican Council highlights, "has always venerated the divine Scriptures as she venerated the Body of the Lord, in so far as she never ceases, particularly in the sacred liturgy, to partake of the bread of life and to offer it to the faithful from the one table of the Word of God and the Body of Christ" (*Dei Verbum*, no. 21). The Council rightly concludes: "Just as from constant attendance at the Eucharistic mystery the life of the Church draws increase, so a new impulse of spiritual life may be expected from increased veneration of the Word of God, which 'stands for ever'" (*Dei Verbum*, no. 26).

> *Homily at Mass for the opening of the twelfth*
> *general assembly of the Synod of Bishops*
> *October 5, 2008*

78. *Bread and Word*

In order to progress on our earthly pilgrimage towards the heavenly Kingdom, we all need to be nourished by the word and the bread of eternal Life, and these are inseparable from one another!

Message for the Twenty-First World Youth Day
February 22, 2006

79. *Capable of loving*

In the Eucharistic celebration it is Christ himself who becomes present among us; indeed, even more: he comes to enlighten us with his teaching—in the Liturgy of the Word—and to nourish us with his Body and his Blood—in the Eucharistic Liturgy and in Communion. Thus, he comes to teach us to love, to make us capable of loving and thereby capable of living.

Homily at Mass in Casa del Marmo,
Rome's prison for minors
March 18, 2007

80. *The Eucharistic Prayer*

It is difficult for the faithful to follow a text as long as our Eucharistic Prayer. For this reason these new "inventions" are constantly cropping up. However, with constantly new Eucharistic Prayers one does not solve the problem. The problem is that this is a moment that also invites others to silence with God and to pray with God. Therefore, things can only go better if the Eucharistic Prayer is said well and with the correct pauses for silence, if it is said with interiority but also with the art of speaking. It follows that the recitation of the Eucharistic Prayer requires a moment of special attention if it is to be spoken in such a way that it involves others. I believe we should also find opportunities in catechesis, in homilies and in other circumstances to explain this Eucharistic Prayer well to the People of God so that they can follow the important moments—the account and the words of the Institution, the prayer for the living and the dead, the thanksgiving to the Lord and the *epiclesis*—if the community is truly to be involved in this prayer. Thus, the words must be pronounced properly. There must then be an adequate preparation. Altar servers must know what to do; lectors must be truly experienced speakers. Then the choir, the singing, should be rehearsed: and let the altar be properly decorated. All this, even if it is a matter of many practical things, is part of the *ars celebrandi*. But to conclude, the fundamental element is this art of entering into communion with the Lord, which we prepare for as priests throughout our lives.

Meeting with priests of the Diocese of Albano, Italy
August 31, 2006

81. *The consecration*

The bread that we break is a communion with the Body of Christ. The cup of blessing which we bless is a communion with the Blood of Christ. This extraordinary revelation comes to us from Christ and has been transmitted to us by the Apostles and by the whole Church for almost two thousand years: Christ instituted the sacrament of the Eucharist on the evening of Holy Thursday. He wanted his sacrifice to be presented anew, in an unbloody manner, every time a priest repeats the words of consecration over the bread and wine. Millions of times over the last twenty centuries, in the humblest chapels and in the most magnificent basilicas and cathedrals, the risen Lord has given himself to his people, thus becoming, in the famous expression of St. Augustine, "more intimate to us than we are to ourselves" (cf. *Confessions*, III, 6, 11).

Homily at Mass in Lourdes
September 13, 2008

82. *On the altar*

On the altar . . . the sacrifice of Christ . . . will be offered every day. On this altar he will continue to sacrifice himself in the sacrament of the Eucharist, for our salvation and for that of the whole world. Jesus makes himself truly present in the Eucharistic Mystery, which is renewed on every altar. His is a dynamic presence that takes hold of us to make us his, to liken us to him. He attracts us with the force of his love, bringing us out of ourselves to be united with him, making us one with him.

Homily at Mass in Albano, Italy
September 21, 2008

83. *The exchange of peace*

Among Christians, the word "peace" has taken on a very particular meaning: it has become a word to designate communion in the Eucharist. There Christ's peace is present. In all the places where the Eucharist is celebrated, a great network of peace spreads through the world. The communities gathered around the Eucharist make up a kingdom of peace as wide as the world itself.

Homily at Midnight Mass for Christmas
December 24, 2005

84. *To altar servers*

Dear Altar Servers, you are, in fact, already apostles of Jesus! When you take part in the Liturgy by carrying out your altar service, you offer a witness to all. Your absorption, the devotion that wells up from your heart and is expressed in gestures, in song, in the responses: if you do it correctly and not absentmindedly, then in a certain way your witness is one that moves people. The Eucharist is the source and summit of the bond of friendship with Jesus. You are very close to Jesus in the Eucharist, and this is the most important sign of his friendship for each one of us. Do not forget it. This is why I am asking you not to take this gift for granted so that it does not become a sort of habit, knowing how it works and doing it automatically; rather, discover every day anew that something important happens, that the living God is among us and that you can be close to him and help him so that his mystery is celebrated and reaches people. If you do not give in to habit, if you put your innermost self into carrying out your service, then you will truly be his apostles and bear fruits of goodness and service in every context of your life: in the family, at school, in your free time.

General Audience
August 2, 2006

85. *Transformation*

We must all work together to celebrate the Eucharist ever more profoundly: not only as a rite, but as an existential process that touches me in the very depths of my being, more than any other thing, and changes me, transforms me. And in transforming me, it also begins the transformation of the world that the Lord desires and for which he wants to make us his instruments.

Meeting with clergy of the Diocese of Rome
February 26, 2009

Participating

86. *Meeting one another*

The Eucharist can never be a private event, reserved for people chosen through affinity or friendship. The Eucharist is a public devotion that has nothing esoteric or exclusive about it. . . . We did not choose to meet one another, we came and find ourselves next to one another, brought together by faith and called to become one body, sharing the one Bread which is Christ.

Homily at Mass on the Solemnity of Corpus Christi
May 22, 2008

87. *Participation in the celebration*

Reception of the Eucharist, adoration of the Blessed Sacrament—by this we mean deepening our Communion, preparing for it and prolonging it—is also about allowing ourselves to enter into communion with Christ, and through him with the whole of the Trinity, so as to become what we receive and to live in communion with the Church. It is by receiving the Body of Christ that we receive the strength "of unity with God and with one another" (St. Cyril of Alexandria, *In Ioannis Evangelium*, 11:11; cf. St. Augustine, *Sermo 577*).

Homily delivered by satellite for the closing of the forty-ninth International Eucharistic Conference in Québec
June 22, 2008

88. *Sacrament of unity*

The Eucharist . . . is the sacrament of unity. Unfortunately, however, Christians are divided, precisely in the sacrament of unity. Sustained by the Eucharist, we must feel all the more roused to striving with all our strength for that full unity which Christ ardently desired in the Upper Room.

Homily at the closing of the twenty-fourth Italian National Eucharistic Congress
May 29, 2005

89. *The road of ecumenism*

The road of ecumenism ultimately points towards a common celebration of the Eucharist (cf. John Paul II, *Ut Unum Sint*, nos. 23-24, 45), which Christ entrusted to his Apostles as the sacrament of the Church's unity par excellence. Although there are still obstacles to be overcome, we can be sure that a common Eucharist one day would only strengthen our resolve to love and serve one another in imitation of our Lord: for Jesus' commandment to "do this in memory of me" (Lk 22:19) is intrinsically ordered to his admonition to "wash one another's feet" (Jn 13:14). For this reason, a candid dialogue concerning the place of the Eucharist—stimulated by a renewed and attentive study of scripture, patristic writings, and documents from across the two millennia of Christian history (cf. *Ut Unum Sint*, nos. 69-70)—will undoubtedly help to advance the ecumenical movement and unify our witness to the world.

Ecumenical meeting in St. Mary's Cathedral, Sydney
July 18, 2008

90. *Participation of the sick*

The Eucharist, distributed to the sick in a dignified and prayerful way, is the vital sap that comforts them and instills in their souls the inner light with which to live the condition of sickness and suffering with faith and hope.

Address to the Pontifical Council for Health Pastoral Care
March 22, 2007

91. *School*

Every Eucharistic celebration is the perennial memorial of the Crucified and Risen Christ, who defeated the power of evil with the omnipotence of his love. It is therefore at the "school" of the Eucharistic Christ that we are granted to learn and to love life always and to accept our apparent powerlessness in the face of illness and death.

Address at the end of Mass on the
feast of Our Lady of Lourdes
February 11, 2009

Adoring

92. *Listening*

Friends, do not be afraid of silence or stillness, listen to God, adore him in the Eucharist.

> *Meeting with young people in Yonkers, New York*
> *April 19, 2008*

93. *The perfect gift*

Contemplating the mystery of the Eucharist, which expresses in a sublime way the free gift of the Father in the Person of his Only Begotten Son for the salvation of mankind, and the full and docile readiness of Christ to drink to the dregs the "cup" of the will of God (cf. Mt 26:39), we can more readily understand how "faith in the divine initiative" models and gives value to the "human response." In the Eucharist, that perfect gift which brings to fulfillment the plan of love for the redemption of the world, Jesus offers himself freely for the salvation of mankind.

> *Message for the Forty-Sixth*
> *World Day of Prayer for Vocations*
> *January 20, 2009*

94. *Recollection*

In life today, often noisy and dispersive, it is more important than ever to recover the capacity for inner silence and recollection. Eucharistic adoration permits this not only centered on the "I" but more so in the company of that "You" full of love who is Jesus Christ, "the God who is near to us."

Angelus
June 10, 2007

95. *Celebration and adoration (1)*

An intrinsic connection exists between celebration and adoration. In fact, Holy Mass is in itself the Church's greatest act of adoration: "No one eats of this flesh," as St. Augustine writes, "without having first adored it" (*Enarr. in Ps. 98,9: CCL* XXXIX, 1385). Adoration outside Holy Mass prolongs and intensifies what has taken place in the liturgical celebration and makes a true and profound reception of Christ possible.

Angelus
June 10, 2007

96. *Celebration and adoration (2)*

After the Council, after a period in which the sense of Eucharistic Adoration was somewhat lacking, the joy of this adoration was reborn everywhere in the Church, as we saw and heard at the Synod on the Eucharist. Of course, the conciliar *Constitution on the Liturgy* enabled us to discover to the full the riches of the Eucharist in which the Lord's testament is accomplished: he gives himself to us and we respond by giving ourselves to him. We have now rediscovered, however, that without adoration as an act consequent to Communion received, this center which the Lord gave to us—that is, the possibility of celebrating his sacrifice and thus of entering into a sacramental, almost corporeal, communion with him—loses its depth as well as its human richness. Adoration means entering the depths of our hearts in communion with the Lord, who makes himself bodily present in the Eucharist. In the monstrance, he always entrusts himself to us and asks us to be united with his Presence, with his risen Body.

Meeting with clergy of the Diocese of Rome
March 2, 2006

97. *Celebration and adoration (3)*

The worship of the Eucharist outside of the Mass, but strictly linked to the celebration, is also of great value for the life of the Church, for it aspires to sacramental and spiritual communion. As John Paul II wrote, "If in our time Christians must be distinguished above all by the 'art of prayer,' how can we not feel a renewed need to spend time in spiritual converse, in silent adoration, in heartfelt love before Christ present in the Most Holy Sacrament?" (*Ecclesia de Eucharistia*, no. 25). From this experience we cannot but receive strength, comfort and support.

Address to the Canadian bishops on their ad limina *visit*
May 11, 2006

98. *Submission and union*

It is appropriate to remember . . . the different meanings of the word "adoration" in the Greek and Latin languages. The Greek word *proskýnesis* means the act of submission, the recognition of God as our true measure and by whose law we agree to abide. The Latin word *adoratio*, on the other hand, denotes the physical contact: the kiss, the embrace which is implicit in the idea of love. The aspect of submission foresees a relationship of union because the one to whom we submit is Love. Indeed, in the Eucharist, worship must become union: union with the living Lord and then with his Mystical Body.

Address to the Congregation for Divine Worship
and the Discipline of the Sacraments
March 13, 2009

99. Question

[What is adoration?] I would say: adoration is recognizing that Jesus is my Lord, that Jesus shows me the way to take, and that I will live well only if I know the road that Jesus points out and follow the path he shows me. Therefore, adoration means saying: "Jesus, I am yours. I will follow you in my life, I never want to lose this friendship, this communion with you." I could also say that adoration is essentially an embrace with Jesus in which I say to him: "I am yours, and I ask you, please stay with me always."

Meeting with children who had received
First Communion that year
October 15, 2005

100. *Union*

The Body and Blood of Christ are given to us so that we ourselves will be transformed in our turn. We are to become the Body of Christ, his own Flesh and Blood. We all eat the one bread, and this means that we ourselves become one. In this way, adoration, as we said earlier, becomes union. God no longer simply stands before us as the One who is totally Other. He is within us, and we are in him. His dynamic enters into us and then seeks to spread outwards to others until it fills the world, so that his love can truly become the dominant measure of the world.

Homily at Mass for the Twentieth World Youth Day
August 21, 2005

101. *Adoration and the poor*

In adoration we look at the consecrated Host, the most simple type of bread and nourishment, made only of a little flour and water. In this way, it appears as the food of the poor, those to whom the Lord made himself closest in the first place.

Homily at Mass on the Solemnity of the
Body and Blood of Christ
June 15, 2006

102. *Believing*

Adoring the Body of Christ means believing that there, in that piece of Bread, Christ is really there, and gives true sense to life, to the immense universe as to the smallest creature, to the whole of human history as to the most brief existence. Adoration is prayer that prolongs the celebration and Eucharistic communion and in which the soul continues to be nourished: it is nourished with love, truth, peace; it is nourished with hope, because the One before whom we prostrate ourselves does not judge us, does not crush us but liberates and transforms us.

Homily at Mass on the Solemnity of Corpus Christi
May 22, 2008

103. *The hidden treasure*

In one of his parables the Lord speaks of a treasure hidden in the field; whoever finds it sells all he has in order to buy that field, because the hidden treasure is more valuable than anything else. The hidden treasure, the good greater than any other good, is the Kingdom of God—it is Jesus himself, the Kingdom in person. In the sacred Host, he is present, the true treasure, always waiting for us. Only by adoring this presence do we learn how to receive him properly—we learn the reality of communion, we learn the Eucharistic celebration from the inside.

Homily at Vespers in Altötting
September 11, 2006

104. *Invitation*

It is important that you make participation in the Eucharist, in which Jesus gives himself for us, the heart of your life. He who died for the sins of all desires to enter into communion with each one of you and is knocking at the doors of your hearts to give you his grace. Go to the encounter with him in the Blessed Eucharist, go to adore him in the churches, kneeling before the Tabernacle: Jesus will fill you with his love and will reveal to you the thoughts of his Heart. If you listen to him, you will feel ever more deeply the joy of belonging to his Mystical Body, the Church, which is the family of his disciples held close by the bond of unity and love.

> *Message to young Catholics of the Netherlands*
> *November 21, 2005*

105. *Precedence*

Adoration must precede our every activity and program, that it may render us truly free and that we may be given the criteria for our action.

> *Address to participants in the fourth*
> *national ecclesial convention of Italy*
> *October 19, 2006*

Eucharistic Devotion

THE *CORPUS DOMINI* [BODY OF THE LORD]

106. *It is Jesus who passes*

Corpus Christi is thus a renewal of the mystery of Holy Thursday, as it were, in obedience to Jesus' invitation to proclaim from "the housetops" what he told us in secret (cf. Mt 10:27). It was the Apostles who received the gift of the Eucharist from the Lord in the intimacy of the Last Supper, but it was destined for all, for the whole world. This is why it should be proclaimed and exposed to view: so that each one may encounter "Jesus who passes" as happened on the roads of Galilee, Samaria and Judea; in order that each one, in receiving it, may be healed and renewed by the power of his love.

Homily at Mass on the Solemnity of Corpus Christi
June 7, 2007

107. *Immersion*

For this reason, the Feast of *Corpus Christi* is characterized particularly by the tradition of carrying the Most Holy Sacrament in procession, an act full of meaning. By carrying the Eucharist through the streets and squares, we desire to immerse the Bread come down from Heaven in our daily lives. We want Jesus to walk where we walk, to live where we live. Our world, our existence, must become his temple. On this feast day, the Christian Community proclaims that the Eucharist is its all, its very life, the source of life that triumphs over death.

Angelus
June 18, 2006

108. *In procession*

The *Corpus Christi* procession teaches us that the Eucharist seeks to free us from every kind of despondency and discouragement, wants to raise us, so that we can set out on the journey with the strength God gives us through Jesus Christ.

Homily at Mass on the Solemnity of Corpus Christi
May 22, 2008

109. *Through the streets and among the houses*

[In the *Corpus Christi* procession] we bring Christ, present under the sign of bread, onto the streets of our city. We entrust these streets, these homes, our daily life, to his goodness. May our streets be streets of Jesus! May our houses be homes for him and with him! May our life of every day be penetrated by his presence. With this gesture, let us place under his eyes the sufferings of the sick, the solitude of young people and the elderly, temptations, fears— our entire life. The procession represents an immense and public blessing for our city: Christ is, in person, the divine Blessing for the world. May the ray of his blessing extend to us all!

Homily on the Solemnity of Corpus Christi
May 26, 2005

110. *The Blessed Sacrament*

The sacred host exposed to our view speaks of this infinite power of Love manifested on the glorious Cross. The sacred host speaks to us of the incredible abasement of the One who made himself poor so as to make us rich in him, the One who accepted the loss of everything so as to win us for his Father. The sacred host is the living, efficacious and real sacrament of the eternal presence of the savior of mankind to his Church.

Meditation during the eucharistic procession in Lourdes
September 14, 2008

VIII. SUNDAY

111. Iuxta dominicam vivere *[living in accordance with the Lord's Day]*

"Living in accordance with the Lord's Day" (St. Ignatius of Antioch) means living in the awareness of the liberation brought by Christ and making our lives a constant self-offering to God, so that his victory may be fully revealed to all humanity through a profoundly renewed existence.

> *Apostolic Exhortation* The Sacrament of Charity
> (Sacramentum Caritatis), *no. 72*
> *February 22, 2007*

112. Sine dominico non possumus *[we cannot live without Sunday]*

For the first Christians, participation in the Sunday celebrations was the natural expression of their belonging to Christ, of communion with his Mystical Body, in the joyful expectation of his glorious return. This belonging was expressed heroically in what happened to the martyrs of Abitene, who faced death exclaiming, "*Sine dominico non possumus*": without gathering together on Sunday to celebrate the Eucharist, we cannot live. How much more necessary it is today to reaffirm the sacredness of the Lord's

Day and the need to take part in Sunday Mass! The cultural context in which we live, often marked by religious indifference and secularism that blot out the horizon of the transcendent, must not let us forget that the People of God, born from "Christ's Passover, Sunday," should return to it as to an inexhaustible source, in order to understand better and better the features of their own identity and the reasons for their existence.

Letter to Cardinal Francis Arinze on the forty-third anniversary of Sacrosanctum Concilium
November 27, 2006

113. Octava dies *[eighth day]*

Sunday was not chosen by the Christian community but by the Apostles, and indeed by Christ himself, who on that day, "the first day of the week," rose and appeared to the disciples [cf. Mt 28:1; Mk 16:9; Lk 24:1; Jn 20:1, 19; Acts 20:7; 1 Cor 16:2], and appeared to them again "eight days later" (Jn 20:26). Sunday is the day on which the Risen Lord makes himself present among his followers, invites them to his banquet and shares himself with them so that they too, united and configured to him, may worship God properly. Therefore, as I encourage people to give ever greater importance to the "Lord's Day," I am eager to highlight the central place of the Eucharist as a fundamental pillar of Sunday and of all ecclesial life. Indeed, at every Sunday Eucharistic celebration, the sanctification of the

Christian people takes place as it will take place until the Sunday that never sets, the day of the definitive encounter of God with his creatures.

Letter to Cardinal Francis Arinze on the forty-third anniversary of Sacrosanctum Concilium
November 27, 2006

114. *Quality*

It is true: our spiritual life essentially depends upon the Eucharist. Without it, faith and hope are extinguished and charity cools. This is why, dear friends, I urge you to take better and better care of the quality of the Eucharistic celebrations, especially those on Sunday, so that Sunday may truly be the Lord's Day and confer fullness of meaning on everyday events and activities, demonstrating the joy and beauty of the faith.

Address to pilgrims from the Diocese of Verona
June 4, 2005

115. *The Sunday precept*

No Christian community can be established if it is not founded and centered in the Eucharistic celebration. . . . Gathered in church to celebrate the Pasch of the Lord, the faithful draw from this Sacrament light and strength in order to live their baptismal vocation to the full. Furthermore, the meaning of the Sacrament does not end with the celebration. In "receiving the Bread of Life, the disciples of Christ ready themselves to undertake with the strength of the Risen Lord and his Spirit the tasks which await them in their ordinary life" (*Dies Domini*, no. 45). Having lived and proclaimed the presence of the Risen One, the faithful will have at heart [the desire] to be evangelizers and witnesses in their daily life.

Address to the bishops of Canada on their ad limina *visit*
May 11, 2006

116. *Reliving*

The disciples of Emmaus recognized [Jesus] and remembered the times when [he] had broken the bread. And this breaking of the bread reminds us of the first Eucharist celebrated in the context of the Last Supper, when Jesus broke the bread and thus anticipated his death and Resurrection by giving himself to the disciples. Jesus also breaks bread with us and for us, he makes himself present with us in the Holy Eucharist, he gives us himself and opens our hearts. In the Holy Eucharist, in the encounter with his Word, we too can meet and know Jesus at this two-fold Table of the Word and of the consecrated Bread and Wine. Every Sunday the community thus relives the Lord's Passover and receives from the Savior his testament of love and brotherly service.

General Audience
March 26, 2008

117. Centrality

Sunday, throughout the Church's life, has been the privileged moment of the community's encounter with the risen Lord. Christians should be aware that they are not following a character from past history, but the living Christ, present in the *today* and the *now* of their lives. He is the living one who walks alongside us, revealing to us the meaning of events, of suffering and death, of rejoicing and feasting, entering our homes and remaining there, feeding us with the bread that gives life. For this reason Sunday Mass must be the center of Christian life. The encounter with Christ in the Eucharist calls forth a commitment to evangelization and an impulse towards solidarity; it awakens in the Christian a strong desire to proclaim the Gospel and to bear witness to it in the world so as to build a more just and humane society. From the Eucharist, in the course of the centuries, an immense wealth of charity has sprung forth, of sharing in the difficulties of others, of love and of justice. Only from the Eucharist will the civilization of love spring forth.

Address at the opening of the Fifth General Conference of
the Bishops of Latin America and the Caribbean
May 13, 2007

118. *The Lord's Day*

Sunday, the Lord's Day, is a favorable opportunity to draw strength from him, the Lord of life. The Sunday precept is not, therefore, an externally imposed duty, a burden on our shoulders. On the contrary, taking part in the Celebration, being nourished by the Eucharistic Bread and experiencing the communion of their brothers and sisters in Christ is a need for Christians, it is a joy; Christians can thus replenish the energy they need to continue on the journey we must make every week.

Homily at the closing of the twenty-fourth
Italian National Eucharistic Congress
May 29, 2005

119. *In the ecclesial community*

Faithful participation in the Sunday Eucharistic celebration helps one to feel a living part of the Ecclesial Community even when one is outside his or her own parish. Wherever we find ourselves, we always need to be nourished by the Eucharist.

Angelus
August 13, 2006

120. *The participation of the family*

[There is a] need to give priority in pastoral programs to appreciation of the importance of Sunday Mass. We must motivate Christians to take an active part in it, and if possible, to bring their families, which is even better. The participation of parents with their children at Sunday Mass is an effective way of teaching the faith and it is a close bond that maintains their unity with one another.

Address at the opening of the Fifth General Conference of
the Bishops of Latin America and the Caribbean
May 13, 2007

121. *Sunday Eucharist and family unity*

Dear parents! I ask you to help your children to grow in faith, I ask you to accompany them on their journey towards First Communion, a journey which continues beyond that day, and to keep accompanying them as they make their way to Jesus and with Jesus. Please, go with your children to church and take part in the Sunday Eucharistic celebration! You will see that this is not time lost; rather, it is the very thing that can keep your family truly united and centered. Sunday becomes more beautiful, the whole week becomes more beautiful, when you go to Sunday Mass together.

Homily at Mass in Munich
September 10, 2006

122. *Awareness*

May all of you become ever more deeply aware of the importance of the Sunday Eucharist, because Sunday, the first day of the week, is the day when we honor Christ, the day when we receive the strength to live each day the gift of God.

Homily delivered by satellite for the closing of the forty-ninth International Eucharistic Conference in Québec June 22, 2008

IX. EUCHARISTIC DIMENSION OF CHRISTIAN LIFE

123. *A gift*

Christianity is first and foremost a gift: God gives himself to us—he does not give something, but himself. And this does not only happen at the beginning, at the moment of our conversion. He constantly remains the One who gives. He continually offers us his gifts. He always precedes us. This is why the central act of Christian being is the Eucharist: gratitude for having been gratified, joy for the new life that he gives us.

Homily at Mass of the Lord's Supper, Holy Thursday
March 20, 2008

124. *Eucharistic center*

The Eucharist—the center of our Christian being—is founded on Jesus' sacrifice for us; it is born from the suffering of love which culminated in the Cross. We live by this love that gives itself. It gives us the courage and strength to suffer with Christ and for him in this world, knowing that in this very way our life becomes great and mature and true.

Homily at Mass for the opening of the Year of St. Paul
June 28, 2008

125. *Lesson*

Especially in the mystery of the Eucharist, we ourselves, our priests and all our faithful can live to the full this relationship with Christ: here he becomes tangible among us, he gives himself ever anew, he becomes ours, so that we may become his and learn his love.

Address to the Italian Bishops' Conference
May 30, 2005

126. *Sacrament of charity*

In the Eucharist Christ wanted to give us *his* love, which impelled him to offer his life for us on the Cross. At the Last Supper, in washing the disciples' feet, Jesus left us the commandment of love: "even as I have loved you, that you also love one another" (Jn 13:34). However, since this is only possible by remaining united to him like branches to the vine (cf. Jn 15:1-8), he chose to remain with us himself in the Eucharist so that we could *remain in him*. When, therefore, we nourish ourselves with faith on his Body and Blood, his love passes into us and makes us capable in turn of laying down our lives for our brethren (cf. 1 Jn 3:16). . . . From this flows Christian joy, the joy of love and the joy to be loved.

Angelus
March 18, 2007

127. *Spiritual worship*

The Church knows that in the Holy Eucharist Christ's gift of himself, his true sacrifice, becomes present. However, the Church prays that the community celebrating may truly be united with Christ and transformed; she prays that we may become what we cannot be with our own efforts: a "rational" offering [cf. Rm 12:1, Vulgate] that is acceptable to God.

General Audience
January 7, 2009

128. *Love in daily life*

The Eucharist can never be just a liturgical action. It is complete only if the liturgical agape then becomes love in daily life. In Christian worship, the two things become one—experiencing the Lord's love in the act of worship and fostering love for one's neighbor. At this hour, we ask the Lord for the grace to learn to live the mystery of the Eucharist ever more deeply, in such a way that the transformation of the world can begin to take place.

Homily at Mass of the Lord's Supper, Holy Thursday
April 9, 2009

129. *Spiritual energy*

In the Eucharist the Lord gives himself to us in his body, soul and divinity, and we become one with him and with others. Our response to his love must then be concrete and expressed in an authentic conversion to love, in forgiveness, in welcoming one another and being attentive to the needs of everyone. The kinds of service that we can render to our neighbor in everyday life, with a bit of attention, are many and varied. The Eucharist thus becomes the source of spiritual energy that renews our life each day, and in this way also renews the world in Christ's love.

Angelus
September 25, 2005

130. *Hospitality*

Having given thanks and praise, the Lord then breaks the bread and gives it to the disciples. Breaking the bread is the act of the father of the family who looks after his children and gives them what they need for life. But it is also the act of hospitality with which the stranger, the guest, is received within the family and is given a share in its life. Dividing (*dividere*), sharing (*condividere*) brings about unity. Through sharing, communion is created.

Homily at Mass of the Lord's Supper, Holy Thursday
April 9, 2009

131. *In communion*

Christ's gift of himself implies the aspiration to attract all to communion in his body, to unite the world. Only in communion with Christ, the exemplary man, one with God, does the world thus become as we all wish it to be: a mirror of divine love. This dynamism is ever present in the Eucharist—this dynamism must inspire and form our life.

General Audience
January 7, 2009

132. *Openness*

"Because there is one bread, we, though many, are one body," says St. Paul (1 Cor 10:17). By this he meant: since we receive the same Lord and he gathers us together and draws us into himself, we ourselves are one. This must be evident in our lives. It must be seen in our capacity to forgive. It must be seen in our sensitivity to the needs of others. It must be seen in our willingness to share. It must be seen in our commitment to our neighbors, both those close at hand and those physically far away, whom we nevertheless consider to be close.

> *Homily at Mass for the Twentieth World Youth Day*
> *August 21, 2005*

133. *Branches*

We celebrate the Eucharist in the awareness that its price was the death of the Son—the sacrifice of his life that remains present in it. Every time we eat this bread and drink this cup, we proclaim the death of the Lord until he comes, St. Paul says (cf. 1 Cor 11:26). But we also know that from this death springs life, because Jesus transformed it into a sacrificial gesture, an act of love, thereby profoundly changing it: love has overcome death. In the Holy

Eucharist, from the Cross, he draws us all to himself (cf. Jn 12:32) and makes us branches of the Vine that is Christ himself. If we abide in him, we will also bear fruit, and then from us will no longer come the vinegar of self-sufficiency, of dissatisfaction with God and his creation, but the good wine of joy in God and of love for our neighbor.

Homily at Mass for the opening of
the Synod on the Eucharist
October 2, 2005

134. *Form*

If the Eucharist becomes the form of our existence, then for us to live is truly Christ and to die is equivalent to passing fully to him and to Trinitarian life in God, where we will also be in full communion with our brethren. "He who eats my flesh and drinks my blood abides in me, and I in him . . . he who eats this bread will live for ever" (Jn 6:56, 58).

Homily at the funeral Mass for
Cardinal Antonio Innocenti
September 10, 2008

135. *Proximity*

Participation in the Eucharist does not distance our contemporaries. On the contrary, since it is the expression par excellence of God's love, it calls us to join forces with all our brothers and sisters to confront today's challenges and make the earth a place that is pleasant to live in.

Homily delivered by satellite for the closing of the forty-ninth International Eucharistic Conference in Québec
June 22, 2008

136. *Active charity*

Anyone nourished with the faith of Christ at the Eucharistic Table assimilates his same style of life, which is the style of service especially attentive to the weakest and most underprivileged persons. In fact, practical charity is a criterion that proves the authenticity of our liturgical celebrations [cf. John Paul II, *Mane Nobiscum Domine*, no. 28].

Angelus
June 19, 2005

137. *The exercise of charity*

The exercise of charity is the culmination and synthesis of the whole of Christian life. The commandment of love—as we well know—is nourished when disciples of Christ, united, share in the banquet of the Eucharist which is, par excellence, the sacrament of brotherhood and love. And just as Jesus at the Last Supper combined the new commandment of fraternal love with the gift of the Eucharist, so his "friends," following in the footsteps of Christ who made himself a "servant" of humanity, and sustained by his Grace, cannot but dedicate themselves to mutual service, taking charge of one another, complying with St. Paul's recommendation: "bear one another's burdens, and so fulfill the law of Christ" (Gal 6:2). Only in this way does love increase among believers and for all people [cf. 1 Thes 3:12].

Message for the Ninety-Fifth
World Day of Migrants and Refugees
August 24, 2008

138. *Contemplation and action*

The Eucharistic mystery is the privileged point of convergence between the various contexts of Christian life, including that of intellectual research. Encountered in the liturgy and contemplated in adoration, Jesus in the Eucharist is like a "prism" through which one can penetrate further into reality, in the ascetic and mystical, the intellectual and speculative, as well as the historical and moral perspectives. In the Eucharist, Christ is really present and Holy Mass is a living memorial of his Pasch. The Blessed Sacrament is the qualitative center of the cosmos and of history. Therefore, it constitutes an inexhaustible source of thought and action for anyone who sets out to seek the truth and desires to cooperate with it. It is, so to speak, a "concentrate" of truth and love. It not only illumines human knowledge, but also and above all human action and human life, in accordance with "the truth in love" (Eph 4:15), as St. Paul said, in the daily task of acting as Jesus himself did. Thus, the Eucharist fosters in those who nourish themselves on it, with perseverance and faith, a fruitful unity between contemplation and action.

Address to teachers and students of Roman universities
December 14, 2006

139. *Solidarity*

The Eucharist is a school of charity and solidarity. The one who is nourished on the Bread of Christ cannot remain indifferent before the one who, even in our day, is deprived of daily bread.

Angelus
May 25, 2008

140. *The desert of the world*

The Eucharist is the indispensable nourishment that sustains [every Christian generation] as they cross the desert of this world, parched by the ideological and economic systems that do not promote life but rather humiliate it. It is a world where the logic of power and possessions prevails rather than that of service and love; a world where the culture of violence and death is frequently triumphant.

Homily at Mass on the Solemnity of Corpus Christi
June 7, 2007

141. *Eucharistic coherence*

Worship pleasing to God can never be a purely private matter, without consequences for our relationships with others: it demands a public witness to our faith. Evidently, this is true for all the baptized, yet it is especially incumbent upon those who, by virtue of their social or political position, must make decisions regarding fundamental values, such as respect for human life, its defense from conception to natural death, the family built upon marriage between a man and a woman, the freedom to educate one's children and the promotion of the common good in all its forms. These values are not negotiable. Consequently, Catholic politicians and legislators, conscious of their grave responsibility before society, must feel particularly bound, on the basis of a properly formed conscience, to introduce and support laws inspired by values grounded in human nature. There is an objective connection here with the Eucharist (cf. 1 Cor 11:27-29). Bishops are bound to reaffirm constantly these values as part of their responsibility to the flock entrusted to them.

Apostolic Exhortation The Sacrament of Charity
(Sacramentum Caritatis), *no. 83*
February 22, 2007

142. *Moral transformation*

The moral urgency born of welcoming Jesus into our lives is the fruit of gratitude for having experienced the Lord's unmerited closeness.

> *Apostolic Exhortation* The Sacrament of Charity
> (Sacramentum Caritatis), *no. 82*
> *February 22, 2007*

The Eucharist and Mission

143. *Gift*

The goal of all [Christian] mission [is] *to bring Christ to others.* Not just a theory or a way of life inspired by Christ, but the gift of his very person.

> *Apostolic Exhortation* The Sacrament of Charity
> (Sacramentum Caritatis), *no. 86*
> *February 22, 2007*

144. *Gift and mystery*

The Eucharist [is] the source of holiness and spiritual nourishment for our mission in the world: this supreme "gift and mystery" manifests and communicates to us the fullness of God's love.

> *Homily at Mass for the conclusion*
> *of the Year of the Eucharist*
> *October 23, 2005*

145. *The Eucharist and evangelization*

The Eucharist, in effect, is the driving force of the Church's entire evangelizing action, a little like the heart in the human body. Christian communities without the Eucharistic celebration, in which one is nourished at the double table of the Word and the Body of Christ, would lose their authentic nature: only those that are "eucharistic" can transmit Christ to humanity, and not only ideas or values which are also noble and important.

Angelus
October 2, 2005

146. *Mission and evangelization*

How very significant is the bond between the Church's mission and the Eucharist. In fact, missionary and evangelizing action is the apostolic diffusion of love that is, as it were, concentrated in the Most Blessed Sacrament. Whoever receives Christ in the reality of his Body and Blood cannot keep this gift to himself, but is impelled to share in courageous witness to the Gospel, in service to brothers and sisters in need, in pardoning offenses. For some, then, the Eucharist is the seed of a specific call to leave all and go to proclaim Christ to those who still do not know him.

Angelus
October 23, 2005

147. *Bread broken*

The Eucharist urges Christians to be "bread broken" for others, to commit themselves to a more just and fraternal world. Even today, faced with the crowds, Christ continues to exhort his disciples, "Give them something to eat yourselves" (Mt 14:16), and in his Name, missionaries proclaim and witness to the Gospel, sometimes with the sacrifice of their lives.

Homily at Mass for the conclusion
of the Year of the Eucharist
October 23, 2005

148. *Holy missionaries*

For the ancient Church, the word "love," *agape*, referred to the mystery of the Eucharist. In this mystery, Christ's love becomes permanently tangible among us. Here, again and again he gives himself. Here, again and again his heart is pierced; here he keeps his promise, the promise which, from the Cross, was to attract all things to himself. In the Eucharist, we ourselves learn Christ's love. It was thanks to this center and heart, thanks to the Eucharist, that the saints lived, bringing to the world God's love in ever new ways and forms.

Homily at Mass for his own installation
in the Chair of Peter
May 7, 2005

149. *Testament*

[In] the Eucharist . . . the Lord's testament is fulfilled: he gives himself to us and we respond by giving ourselves to others, for love of him.

Meeting with young people in Luanda, Angola
March 21, 2009

INDEX

*(Numbering refers to the sequential
positioning of each thought.)*

OTHER TITLES *in the Spiritual Thoughts Series*

Pope Benedict XVI offers inspiration and encouragement through this collection of titles in the Spiritual Thoughts Series.

St. Paul
No. 7-053, 128 pp.

Mary
No. 7-054, 172 pp.

The Saints
No. 7-055, 164 pp.

Family
No. 7-075, 107 pp.

The Word of God
No. 7-065, 100 pp.

The Priesthood
No. 7-086, 96 pp.

Following Christ
No. 7-056, 132 pp.

To order these resources or to obtain a catalog of other USCCB titles, visit *www.usccbpublishing.org* or call toll-free 800-235-8722. In the Washington metropolitan area or from outside the United States, call 202-722-8716. Para pedidos en español, llame al 800-235-8722 y presione 4 para hablar con un representante del servicio al cliente en español.